FINDING DEATH ROW

PEN PALS

By Muriel Agostini

Dont worry, for the most part, they aren't going anywhere...

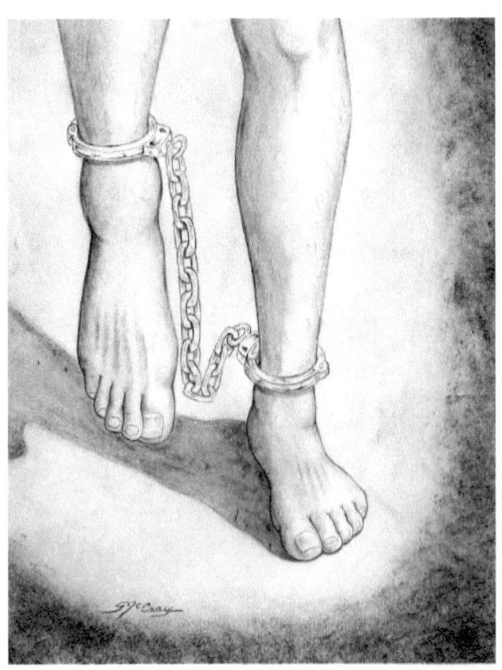

An Instructional Guide and shared journal with tips from Death Row to help you write to Inmates.

This book is for entertainment purposes, if writing to inmates, do so of your own free will and choice.

To,
All of those who wish
to write to an Inmate,
but don't know where
to start. I will share
with you my journey
and give you a place to
start your own.

A special thank you to those who wrote me back, once, twice or if you are one of the few I still write and keep in touch with. With out all of you I would have never thought to put this together. If you see this please stay safe and take care until next time.

I also want to thank my family and friends for sticking by me and Chad at Offbeat Oddities and Collectibles.

There are a few
things you need to
do prior to just
writing to an
inmate, on
Death Row, a lifer or
in General Pop.
At least for those you have never spoken to
before.

THINGS WE WILL GO OVER.

Why do I want to write?

Who do I want to write?

Where do I want to write?

How do I find someone to write?

Finding correct Address for writing

Do's and Dont's and advice from Killers

What I expect from writing

Sample Letters

What will I do with the letters I get back?

Organizations

Artwork

Clips from my personal letters

MISC. INFO. AND JOURNALING SECTION

WHY I WANT TO WRITE DEATH ROW & KILLERS

I want to know who these people are.

Are they all monsters?

Do they have a human side?

Will they even write me back?

Will they tell me they are innocent?

Can I make a connection with someone who did something so horrible they will never be free again?

I want to see if they will lie to me about anything or everything.

I want to see if i can trust anything they say.

WHAT I HAVE FOUND IN WRITING

They are everyone.

Some are monsters!

They do have a human side, some it comes and goes

Yes, some will write back, they might not say what you want to hear but they will write.

Some will say they are innocent. (and may very well be)

Yes I can make a connection.

They will lie! Not all of them but they will lie!

In time, I have made friends out of pen pals, and you just might also.

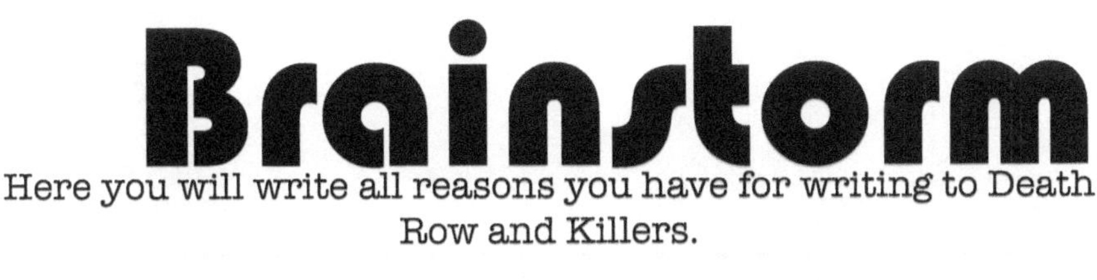

Here you will write all reasons you have for writing to Death Row and Killers.

Brainstorm

6'0"
5'0"
4'0"

Brainstorm

Brainstorm

MY EXCUSES

- I don't really want them to know where I live.

- What if they are total perverts!

- I never really thought about it.

- I bet it is a lot of work

- Where do I start?

AND NOW

THE REALITY TO ALL MY EXCUSES!

THEY DONT KNOW WHERE I LIVE! I USE A DIGITAL MAIL BOX, AND FORWARD MAIL TO BE POSTMARKED.

SOME OF THEM ARE TOTAL PERVERTS!

WELL IM THINKING ABOUT IT NOW!

ITS NOT THAT MUCH WORK

THE INTERNET! OR IN YOUR CASE, RIGHT HERE.

YOUR

EXCUSES

YOUR

EXCUSES

AND

now

AND

now

YOU ARE NOT ALONE

Once you figure out what you want out of letter writing, one letter, a long-term commitment, or a high profile piece of history you can start your own process.

There are many reasons people wish to communicate with Men and Women on Death Row. No matter what your reason is, someone else probably feels the same way. The following are true statements from others who wish to speak to and write to Killers currently serving time.

"Im fascinated by why people's minds work like they do and how are people born to want to or hurt animals and people, what makes them want to do such things"
Trisha L.

"Because I was left for dead by someone whom I guess would be considered a serial killer and I just want to understand"
Heather B.

"I just feel bad for them, they will spend so much time just waiting for the end and knowing it is coming has to be hard"
Andy S.

"I just wanna see if that guy who killed like fifty prostitutes, it would be cool to have a letter from him."
George S.

"Because I know what it is like to love someone who is in prison, they were never mean or bad to me, they were human and did bad things, sometimes knowing the true person can make one see that"
Sandy M.

"I want to help them, I don't know how but maybe just writing a few of them will help in some way. You know give them something else to think about for a little bit."
Stacey R.

" I don't know if I could really befriend someone on Death Row, what if they convince me they didn't do it but they did, and now I feel bad for them? If it weren't for that I would totally do it."
Thomas E.

"I want to know if they will admit what they did, and tell me why. I just want to know why really and if they even care about or feel bad for what they did."
Felicia T.

"I would write to everyone on Death Row if I could, I would go visit them if they let me, I want to know what went so wrong in their life that they made the choices they did to wind up where they are now."
Jan S.

"I don't think everyone on Death
Row is guilty, I think some of them
are there and should not be, so I
hope that I can find one that is not
supposed to be there and help before
it is to late"
Sonia N.

I think they should be there, and I want to
know that they are miserable and how bad
it sucks, I don't wanna have one write to me
and tell me how nice it is."
Mike R.

" I just like the shock
factor of it all, I tell
my friends I like true
crime stuff and the
freak out and tell me
I am crazy, I find it
funny."
Bobby D.

What do your family and friends think about you writing to inmates on Death Row?

For me, it is mixed, some of my family is 100% for it, and others are not at all for it. My mother for one was not at all for me writing to anyone in prison. However my grandmother finds it very interesting and is proud of me. If you write to inmates on Death Row, you may have people in your life that do not agree with your decision. There are even inmates who will tell you not to write to inmates!

people in need: I must advise you that it's not wise to write strangers in prison. I've been in here too long and seen too many weirdos, perverts, sick and sadistic people in here. You don't know what you may be chancing yourself into.

Opinions

Opinions

Opinions

GETTING PAST OPINIONS

How you will move past others opinions or your thoughts on those opinions.

GETTING PAST OPINIONS

WHO DO I WANT TO WRITE TO... (and who i dont)

- I had no clue! I didn't even know where to start.I understand some inmates have backlogs of mail they may not have gotten around to.

- I want someone who would write back.

- Someone who is interesting.

- Someone who will tell me what they did and why.

- I want lots of people to write to.

- I want to write to every incarserated Serial Killer still alive!

- I DON'T want to write anyone who has hurt or killed a child.

- I DON'T want to write to.... (who am I kidding thats my only DON'T)

Write all the types of people you wish to write.

Or if you have a specific person/people in mind add those names.

5'0"
4'0"

Who?

Make sure to write down those types you do NOT want to reach out to!

Who Not!

Depending on what you want from writing to Death Row or any Inmate, it may take time to get there. Are you up for a long term commitment? Do you just want to have a letter from Death Row? Do you want to find someone you can connect with and have a real friendship? Or are you just looking for the dirty details?

It took me a while to figure out what I really wanted with my writing, I will tell you this, at first I just wanted to see if anyone would write me back, and if so what they had to say. With writing I have learned that you never know what you will get back in a letter. I have gotten the dirty details, friendship, many letters from death row and unexpected advice. You can research these Men/Women till you are blue in the face, but none of that will tell you what to expect.

For me, I have found friendship where I did not expect to find them. I have gotten more information about Death Row than I ever would have know. I have been given direction for writing and how to improve my chances of getting letters back. For me one of the most interesting letters I received is, a detailed letter from non other than B.T.K. explainign what he looks for and how he decides to write people back.

WHERE DO I WISH TO WRITE? (near or far)

What prison locations even have
Death Row?
Easy enough Search the wonderful
Internet!

COLOR IN ALL THE STATES YOU WRITE TO!

Remember every state may opt out of the Death
Penalty at any time, just because a state is list-
ed here does not mean that state still has Death
Row.

- Alabama
- Arizona
- Arkansas
- California
- Florida
- Georgia
- Idaho
- Indiana
- Kansas
- Kentucky
- Louisiana
- Mississippi
- Missouri
- Montana
- Nebraska
- Nevada
- New Hampshire

- New Mexico
- North Carolina
- Ohio
- Oklahoma
- Oregon
- Pennsylvania
- South Carolina
- South Dakota
- Tennessee
- Texas
- Utah
- Virginia
- Wyoming
- Federal
- US Military

Well that's a lot of options! I picked a few states; I had no clue who is even going to write me back! For me it didnt matter near or far, as i decided to use a virutal mail box. This is similar to a PO BOX, but it can be anywhere, your mail can be scanned in for you or forwarded to you. You always want to double check all these states still have Death Row!

WRITING MORE THAN ONE

I have come to learn, that most inmates prefer to be the only one you are writing to ESPECIALLY in the same facility!

You can start with one, and go from there! Or you can start with many and narrow down your search! You have choices in who you write to! But remember they do not have to accept your letters! They can refuse mail, just like you can refuse to write back!

If you write multiple inmates and inform those you write you are doing so, be prepared to potentially not have any kind of meaningful conversations with the inmates of your choosing!

They may stop writing, or change the way they write you to encourage you to stop writing, and lastly they may try to take advantage of you, asking for money, photos or anything they may be allowed to receive!

You can write or not write about any and everything you wish! Just remember some things you write may change the way an inmate decides to correspond with you!

I have had Inmates change the way they write to me, and also refuse my letters if I say something they did not like or agree with. So this is something to be prepaired for.

MY DEATH ROW 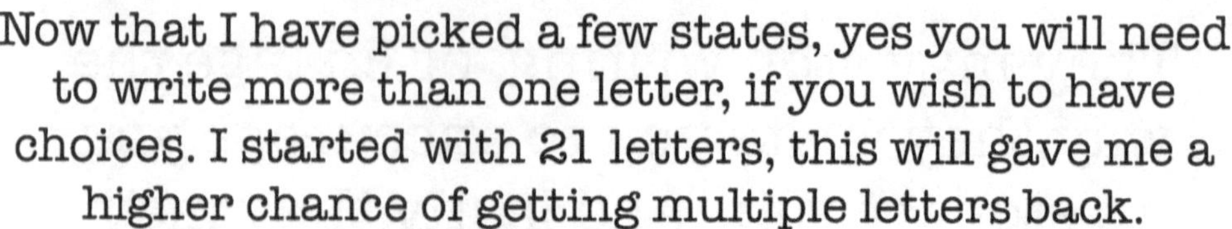 CHOICES

Now that I have picked a few states, yes you will need to write more than one letter, if you wish to have choices. I started with 21 letters, this will gave me a higher chance of getting multiple letters back.

Texas

California

Florida

Ohio

Federal

Arizona

Ohio

Alabama

North Carolina

Kansas (yes this is not a death row state)

These seem to me like some of the more popular states that have the Death Penalty. As well as places I know Inmates I would like to write are located.

PLACES YOU WILL WRITE

Here you will write out places you would like to write as well any hesitation for writing close to home or specific prisons.

WHY THESE PLACES?

There was something on the news about them?

I know someone there.

Its a cool state.

Thats the death row state

NOW THAT I HAVE MY STATES PICKED OUT! FINDING PEN PALS!

- Preform an Internet search for the state of your choice followed by Death Row Inmates.

- Texas was my choice, when you hit enter; it will bring up many things. The first search result that popped up was Texas Dept. of Corrections site that will had a complete list of Death Row inmates for the state of Texas.

- So I took a scroll threw the inmates, click on their names to get more information and picked out a few. There was a lot of information including their convictions.

TEXAS DEATH ROW INMATES

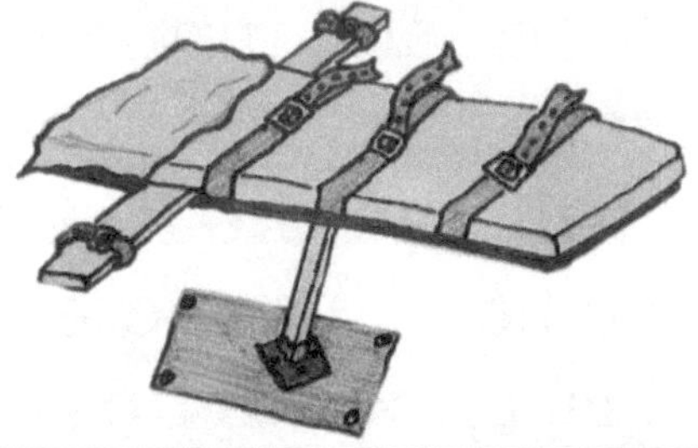

Texas Offenders on Death Row -

When i click on the Texas Offenders on Death Row a Huge
list showed up! Along with the following information.

TDCJ Number   Link   Last Name   First Name   DOB   Gender

Race   Date Received   County   Date of Offense

You want to take note of the Full name, and in this case
TDCJ Number. No matter what state you want to take note
of the Inmate ID number.

What is the inmate ID number? The inmate ID number is
what identifies them in the prison system. It is the number
the Department of Corrections or Federal Bureau of Prisons
uses to identify an inmate in all of their personal paperwork,
and it is used for all prison operations that the inmate is
involved in.

COLLECTING INFO.

When you click on each inmates name or number, it will take you to a new page. This is where you will find the facility, their crimes they have been convicted of, as well as things like Prison write ups or "Infractions" These are all things to look at if you do not wish to make contact with people with certain convictions. Along with the inmate ID # you also want to take note of what facility they are in.

Who would be a good candidate for my writings? Someone I have never heard of before, those who may have been on death row more than 10 years, and those who have only been there for a year or so.

Some newer death row inmates depending on how much press coverage they have received, may have a back log of mail already, others may not get any.

I'll even give you a few Serial Killers, fill in the blanks!

Name	Inmate #	Crime	Facility
Gary	#866218	The _____ River Killer	High security Federal Prison, Florence CO
Rader	#0083707	B_K	El Dorado CF- Central El Dorado KS
David B	Can you find it?	Son of _____	Sullivan Correctional Fallsburg NY
Bianchi	#266962	Who is it?	Walla Walla WA

Research before writing! Some of these guys do not write anymore, can you find out why?

Name	Inmate #	Crime	Facility

Name	Inmate #	Crime	Facility

Name	Inmate #	Crime	Facility

Name	Inmate #	Crime	Facility

Name	Inmate #	Crime	Facility

Name	Inmate #	Crime	Facility

Name	Inmate #	Crime	Facility

Name	Inmate #	Crime	Facility

The aver- age amount of time an inmate spends on death row prior to ex- ecution is 16 years! Some states that is a much higher number!

Now with the inmates on death row, you must remember there judgment day is not set in stone, they have appeals and processes they must go thru prior to execution. There are also states that have death row inmates that have not executed anyone in years.

Ok, I have my list of Death Row Inmates, I have decided I'm really going to do this! Now I need addresses!

When I searched inmates I took note of the facility they are housed in. With this information I went on and did an internet search. "Name of Facility followed by, Inmate mailing address. You want to look thru the internet results to verify you are writing down the correct address. Here are some I started with.

Men's Facilities

California
San Quentin State Prison

(Inmate Name)(Inmate #)
San Quentin State Priosn
San Quentin, CA 94974

Ohio
Chillicothe Correctional Institution

(Inmate Name)(Inmate #)
15802 OH-104
Chillicothe, OH 45601

Texas
Polunsky Unit

(Inmate Name)(Inmate #)
3872 FM 350
Livingston, TX 77351

Women's Facilities

California
Central California Women's Facility

CCWF
(Inmate Name)(Inmate #)
PO Box 1508

Chowchilla, CA 93610

Texas
Mountain View Unit

(Inmate Name)(Inmate #)
Mountain View Unit
2305 Ransom Road
Gatesville, TX 76528

VERIFY ALL ADDRESS PRIOR TO SENDING LETTERS
TO MAKE SURE THEY ARE GOING TO THE CORRECT
PLACE AND NOTHING IS MISSING

The following pages are for you to keep track of any and all addresses you plan on using or want to save for later.

Name And Inmate #	Address
Name And Inmate #	**Address**

Name And Inmate #	Address
Name And Inmate #	Address

Name And Inmate #	Address
Name And Inmate #	Address

Name And Inmate #	Address
Name And Inmate #	Address

Name And Inmate #	Address
Name And Inmate #	Address

Name And Inmate #	Address

Name And Inmate #	Address

Name And Inmate #	Address

I have a binder full of lists of inmates. It is hard to figure out who to write to, or who to write to first. It is ok to make lists. You may not ever write to everyone on those lists, and that is okay. For me it took time to find the right people to write to.

I still have lists, that doesn't mean I will never write them. But for now I am happy with those I write to. I have a feeling I have made lifelong friends, and it all started with a list. A random list of inmates spread out across the country.

POLUNSKY UNIT
3872 FM 350 SOUTH
LIVINGSTON, TX 77351

P.O. Box 5500
Chillicothe, OH
45601

Union Correctional Institution
P.O. Box 1000
Railford, FL 32083

4285 MAIL SERVICE CENTER
RALEIGH, NC 27699

U.S. Penitentiary
P.O. Box 33
Terre Haute, IN 47808

CSP- San Quentin
San Quentin, CA
94974

DO'S AND DONT'S WHEN WRITING TO ANY INMATE!

Make sure you have stamps! Plain paper, lined is fine, unless you have already researched what you can and cannot send to an inmate, you should start with a black pen and plain paper.

Do NOT Send Stamps to an Inmate without verifying they can have them. Most prisons do not allow this! If you want to know what you can and cant sent, you can contact the prison mailroom, or do an internet search to see what is allowed for that facility!

Before sticking that envelope in the mail, remember some Inmates will lie to you, they will tell you what they think you want to hear, they will attempt to manipulate you. You may start getting letters that just take you away and make you forget who you are writing to.

These are things I prepared myself for prior to writing my first letter.

애!

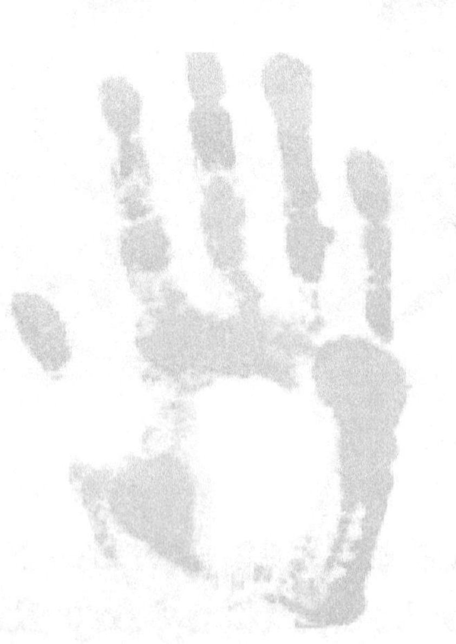

BEFORE I FORGET WE SHOULD GO OVER PICTURES

If you plan on sending photos to any inmate, here are some things you want to keep in mind.

Make sure you write there name and DOJ (Department of Justice) number on the back of the photo!

Photos should never contain things such as nudity, or be sexually suggestive.

There is a very good chance; prison officials will discard photos that are deemed inappropriate before it even reaches the inmate.

Some prisons restrict the size of photos received to 4"x 6"

So you want to check with the individual prison prior to sending photos.

There are also limits to the amount of photos someone can receive at one time. This would be something else to check with each facility.

Make sure your envelope is sufficient for the photos, adding tape or glue to seal the envelope can also cause the photos to not make it to the inmate.

Images that could incite or anger an inmate should be avoided.

Polaroid's and two sided sheets of paper, (anything that can be peeled apart) for the most part is not allowed. Contraband, can be hidden within the photos or paper.

Gang signs, tattoos or potential animal abuse may be discarded.

Any images containing drugs, alcohol, tobacco, or related paraphernalia may be discarded.

Any photos or drawings, containing maps, blueprints or any physical makeup of the prison the image is being sent to may be discarded.

Any images that show construction of tools to assist with a prison break or prison break instruction may be discarded.

Any photos of the inmate themselves or any other inmates may not be allowed.

Any images that may promote any criminal behavior whatsoever are not permitted.

There are a LOT of rules when writing to an inmate!
Be sure to check
what the rules are
at each prison you
write, to insure the
letters are recived!

The following pages are Do's and Dont's and Tips from my personal letters from Death Row and Killers!

" DON'T write a lot of guys
in this facility alone, I'd
rather you write me alone
here. "

" It's not good to write multiple prisoners, especially to the same state or prison Cause it
causes problems, drama and even violence.
Other inmates get jealous and will lie on the
other to get ya'll to stop writing, helping or
seeing others. "

"If you are not going to
continue writing long term
please do not write back"

" Its hard to get yall to give us a chance so if
we see red flags we wont write back. "

" Its not good to bring up that you write others cause MOST wont write back knowing the issues it can cause, they have dealt with it or think you are a groupie, and you don't want that because they will let their friends write and try to get as much as they can out of you cause they don't see you as a serious Pen Pal/Friend. "

" Don't ask others about me, get
to know me and how I treat you
and don't go on what others
say. "

" If you would have wrote me just asking a bunch of questions years ago I would have just told you to FUCK OFF and don't write back! "

"Keep in mind when you started Writing prison, it is a whole
different ball game, for some
that is all it is, a game. And for
some it's a way to leave here for
a few minutes, and friendship
can be found."

"Try not to write two
inmate at the same
prison!"

"Most inmates will go off your first letter
and look for Key Things or Red Flags,
but most will at least write back to see
what you look like and get more information before deciding to continue writing."

"When people write
and straight up say
they write to others,
most wont even waist
the time, paper, ink or
stamp."

" A LOT of women write men on Death
Row to get love letters or feel better
about themselves, since guys in here
aint seen a woman in so long, anyone
will look good to them. "

"Don't share my let-
ters with people, what
I say to you is not for
everyone else to see"

"When you write to people here,
at some point they will ask you for
money"

"I don't always get
all of my mail, so if
you don't hear from
me for a while, write
again they might not
have given it to me"

"I cant always answer all of your
questions our mail is checked here
both what you send in and what I
send out"

"If you write to multi-
ple people here, don't
tell them anything
about me, or even that
you write me at all."

"You must always put your name and return address on the outside of every envelope"

"NO stickers on the letter or envelopes"

"NO Paper, pens, pencils, envelopes, food, clothes, books, magazines can be sent NONE!"

"NO glitter pens! NO glue at all. They will not give me the letters!"

"You shouldn't write
to prisoners they are a
bunch of weirdo's, per-
verts, sick and sadistic
people in here."

"I'm advising you out of Gods love
and respect for you Please don't
write anymore prisoners."

"For some of us letters
coming in is just a way
to escape in our minds
for a little bit so have
your friends write to"

YOU ARE THE WRITER, YOU HAVE AS MUCH CONTROL AS THEY
DO, YOU CAN WRITE OR NOT WRITE WHO EVER YOU WISH! YOU
CAN FOLLOW THEIR RULES OR NOT IT IS 100% YOUR CHOICE.
YOU CAN TERMINATE ANY PEN PAL RELATIONSHIP AT ANY
TIME BY CONTACTING THE PRISON AND REQUESTING NO FUR-
THER CONTACT FROM AN INMATE! BUT REMEMBER THEY CAN
CHOOSE TO REFUSE YOUR LETTERS AS WELL.

Its always good to check with each prison for rules on mail.

If and when you write to Death Row, there may be advice given to you that you would like to remember.

So here is somewhere to write it down!

ADVICE

ADVICE

SAMPLE LETTERS

Here is where I will share with you sample letters I have written for Death Row inmates, Killers and Serial Killers.

Dear,   *Date*

I do not know if you get a lot of mail, if you do, now if you would like you have one more person to write to. But if you do not I hope my letters bring you something to look forward to, as I plan to write you for as long as you would like. I do not know much about you other than why you are on Death Row, but that does not tell me who you are, who you really are. Nor does it tell me who you were prior to you being on Death Row. What did you enjoy doing, where did you like to go? I would like to know any and everything you wish to tell me.

About me, I am ________________, I'm from, ________________ and I am _____ years old. Some of the things I like to do are

____
____
____
____
____

For work I ____________________, and I am writing to you because ____
___________________ I hope that is ok. This is my first letter to you I hope of many, and I would like to ask you a few questions too, if that is ok. If you don't answer them (all) That is ok too.

____
____
___________________________ Until next time take care!

Your Friend,
Xxxxxxxxxx

Return address here

This is the format for the first batch of letters I sent out.

If you plan on writing multiple inmates, making a personalized sample letter, will help you to get letters out faster, as well as keep you on the topics you wish to talk about on your first letter!

The following letter is the sample that I wote and sent out. I got a great results using this format for the more unknown inmates on Death Row.

I don't know if you get much mail.
if you do, now you have one more person
to communicate with and if you don't
I hope my letters bring you something
to look forward to. I don't know
much about you, sure I could look on
the internet but it will just be one
sided stories and reports I could
read that crap all day and still
not know one thing about you, the
real you. What did you enjoy doing?
Where did you like to go? Do you have
a favorite color or food? What would
you be doing if you weren't trapped
behind those walls? Would you have
done anything differently in your life
if you could? I want to know any
and everything you wish to tell me!
Is there anything you look forward to
now? going outside, mail? I'm not
sure what you can do, but do you
enjoy reading, writing, drawing?
I spend a lot of time on computers
so I prefer pen and paper when possible

<h1 align="center">side two</h1>

Has covid changed things for you?
Things outside those walls are crazy.
anywhere you go, you have to wear
a mask, there is hand sanitizer
everywhere. People don't just walk up
and talk to you, everyone keeps away.
except for kids they don't get it
I just feel like if I can smack you
you are to close! But I prefer
my alone time and space, So I
kinda like it. It's strange and
new but it's becoming the normal
I'm looking forward to hearing
from you. So until then take care!

Sincerly,

Return Address

Some inmates will
not write back if it
is not on the letter.

YOUR SAMPLE LETTERS

Here you will plan out your letters, what to write about, current topics and so on.

Current Events, Sports, Weather, Your daily life, are all good
starting topics. You have to remember they live every day in
the same situation in the same place, doing the exact same
thing. There is no change so inmates like to know about the
world outside.
Current events are a good way to see the history that goes
alone with each letter!

____

____

____

____

____

____

____

____

____

____

____

____

____

____

FOLD UP YOUR HANDWRITTEN SAMPLE LETTER
AND KEEP IT HERE.
____

YOUR SAMPLE LETTERS

YOUR SAMPLE LETTERS

Now, I have written many many letters, and not everyone has written me back. So for those I really want to hear from, I keep writting. Every few weeks I send out another letter, in the hopes that one day they will write back. By doing so, I have heard back from one of the people I was most interested in hearing from.

Not only have i gotten a letter back from this person, he explained to me how he decides who to write back. He also graded my original letters and sent them back to me with his letter.
The following are parts of my frist two original letters to BTK, with his gradings.

Dear Dennis,

I'm sure you get lots of mail →hate mail, love mail, fan mail. But incase you don't and this finds its way to you. I hope it finds you well At last as well as it could all things considerd. Sure there is a bunch of information on the internet about you, but its all one sided and about the crimes you have been convicted of. I could read that crap all day long and it wont tell me anything about who you really are. Like what did you enjoy outside of the walls? Do you have a favorite childhood memory? Or place you liked to go? What's your favorite food, color animal? Knowing what you know now would you change anything about your life? If you weren't trapped behind those walls what would you want to be doing now? What do you miss the most? Do you enjoy reading, writing, drawing? Do you have questions about the world beyond the walls and fences?

The side notes are not all legible as Dennis Rader's hand-writing has gone downhill over the years. Things that he has written and underlined he did not like. Sad face in the Q for questions. What i learned from this is to make sure to talk about yourself also. DO NOT just ask questions.

I don't assume to think the food is good!
But is anything decent or enjoyable?
Are there things you look forward to?
I know it's a lot of questions I hope
that in time I can learn about you.
the real you. not just what others
say and think about you.
Out beyond the walls the world
is a crazy place! Before you couldn't
go inside anywhere with a mask because
they thought you were gonna rob them. Now
if your not wearing one they wont let you in!
I went to a cute little antique
store and the older lady was selling
masks with skulls on it, the one I had
was plain black, so I got it.
Just going into the store was crazy,
No one else was there, She had to let
me in, the door was locked. Its all just
strange and new I guess. Looking
forward to hearing from you. Until then
Take Care

Learn from my mistakes when writing your first letter!

Things that were pointed out to me.

- To many questions!
- The word Crap
- The use of the word Gonna
- No return address on the letter
- I did not add the date to the letter

As Far as he, was concerned, my first
letter did not deserve a response.
It was put with the rest of the letters
that were "NO GOOD" or did not deserve a
response.

Of course I had no idea, a few weeks went
by and I sent a second letter.

My second letter was much better as you
can see! As he took time out of his day, to
find and pull out my first letter, as well as
write back. He answered all of my questions, some right on the letters themselfs,
he drew little doodles on both my letters
to him and his letters to me, and most im-
portantly to me, he took the time to tell me
about all I did wrong in the first letter and
the things he looks for.

Dear Dennis,
    hi! I am not sure if you
have gotten my prior letters. I hope
you are! I hope this one finds you
well. I am sure you get a lot of
mail and it takes time to get thru
it all. And I'm sure you get a lot
of questions. I have a few maybe not
ones you normally get. 1st how are
you? Are you well, in good health?
I hope so. 2nd how are you emotionally?
I cant imagine what life is like on
the inside. I hope your emotional
well being is good. 3rd how has life
changed since COVID? has it? Are
they doing all they can to protect
you from this virus? I hope so.
    Now for me...
I'm Muriel I live in Idaho, I'm 28
no kids, I live with my roomie Sammy,
she's great! I'm in pretty good health,
and try to keep healthy. COVID hasn't
changed much for me, I like to be
home so the world hasn't changed
in my apartment.

Again, the side notes are not all legible as Dennis Rader's handwriting has gone downhill over the years. The side notes are the answers that match where he highlighted the questions!

I do find myself cleaning more, But other than that it's pretty normal. When I do go out I have to wear a mask and I stay away from people. I like art and drawing. I'm not great at it, but I like it. I do have nerve issues in my hand so some days are harder to write or draw. How do you pass the time? Do you have any hobbies? Reading, writing, art? I would be happy just knowing you are getting my letters Until next time stay safe and take care.

Sincerly,
Muriel W.

Here I will point out that as he has, if you use a virtual mailbox of any sort that is not in your general area, the post mark will give away where the letters are coming from. The way around this is to send the letters first to the PostMaster of the City your choice. (I send them to a friend out of state who then sends them off for me.) Using one outside of your actual location or where your digital mailbox is located is a good way to protect your physical location.

THINGS YOU DID NOT LIKE ABOUT MY LETTERS BTK ALREADY GRADED ME WHY NOT YOU TOO!

LETTER GRADING

LETTER GRADING

Now, when I started writing I did not expect to hear back from Serial Killers! Which is why i wrote to Killers of all kinds. I have heard from so many different kinds of killers, some have told me their truth in the crimes that were commited. Others have told me they were set up or rail roaded. I tend to take from each one something different, I am finding some truths in each letter. If you decide to do this and really write to people who have taken a life.
Take from it as much or as little as you wish, but know these
men/women are in prison with nothing but time on their hands. They can perfect what they say to everyone who writes them, see what is going to get them the response they are looking for, and find ways to
manipulate you into sending money, photos, taking phone calls, doing things for them outside of the walls, and so on. So REMEMBER, you are in control, you can stop these communications at any time! You do not have to do anything an inmate tells you to do!

Now, I am going to share with you some things that I have been told by my Killer Pen Pals! (One or two I now consider friends) These are exact quotes.

it is Awful it is completly Awful
Behind these walls we Are treated
like Animal's worse than Animals
At least animals Get some companions
And love affection I Get none!

Please allow me to profoundly apologize for
my LATE reply... I was literally 1 month
away from Texas MURDERING me! YUP!
John R

I am a mentor, friend, father figure, but
not a father, but most important I have
not arrived as a man or all that Jesus
is molding me to be.
Jimmy D.

Rader informed me, that it is the third letter that really lets him know who someone is.

It's nice to have someone actually interested in me as a human being and not just look at me like some kind of monster.

Roman A.

From my observations, people get into these "friendship" relationships to serve their own self-interest.

Richard F.

There are guys in here who will do some messed up stuff, I will always be honest with you, if you have questions just ask. Im not like the rest of these guys. I'll always be real with you.

(name withheld)

I dont like to see people pick on the weaker people in the world. When one is a position of strength it is their responsibility to look out for those unfortunate people who cant take care of themselfs.

James D.

At the moment we are on quarantine,
Johnny Sacs (brown bag) for breakfast
lunch and dinner. PB&J and a meat
sandwich in each bag.

Brandon M.

What got me trapped in these
walls was that I shouldn't have
been there, I tried to seek comfort
from a prostitute, but I was being
set up to get robbed.

(name withheld)

ORGANIZATIONS

One of my writers gave me these resources as far as places and organizations that do good for Death Row.

Here are two Death Penalty Resourses that might help you

Death Penalty Info Center
1701 K. Street NW Suite 205
Washington, DC 20006

Deathpenaltyinfo.org

National Coalition to Abolish the Death Penalty
80 M. Street SE
Washington, DC 20003

NCADP.ORG

And
Google: Anti Death Row Groups

Here are are few that were easy to find!

Amnesty International.

The Innocence Project. National Coalition to Abolish the Death Penalty.

American Civil Liberties Union (ACLU)

Conservatives Concerned About the Death Penalty.

HERE YOU WILL WRITE OUT ANY OR-GANIZATIONS YOU HAVE FOUND THAT CAN ASSIST YOU WITH ANYTHING YOU MAY NEED ASSISTANCE WITH!

ORGANIZATIONS

ORGANIZATIONS

ORGANIZATIONS

ARTWORK

Done by Frank "Young Blood" McCray, an amazing artist and friend

Young Blood has been on death row since 2005, He has used art as a form of com-munication since a young age. The copies of his work do not show the true beauty of the work itself.

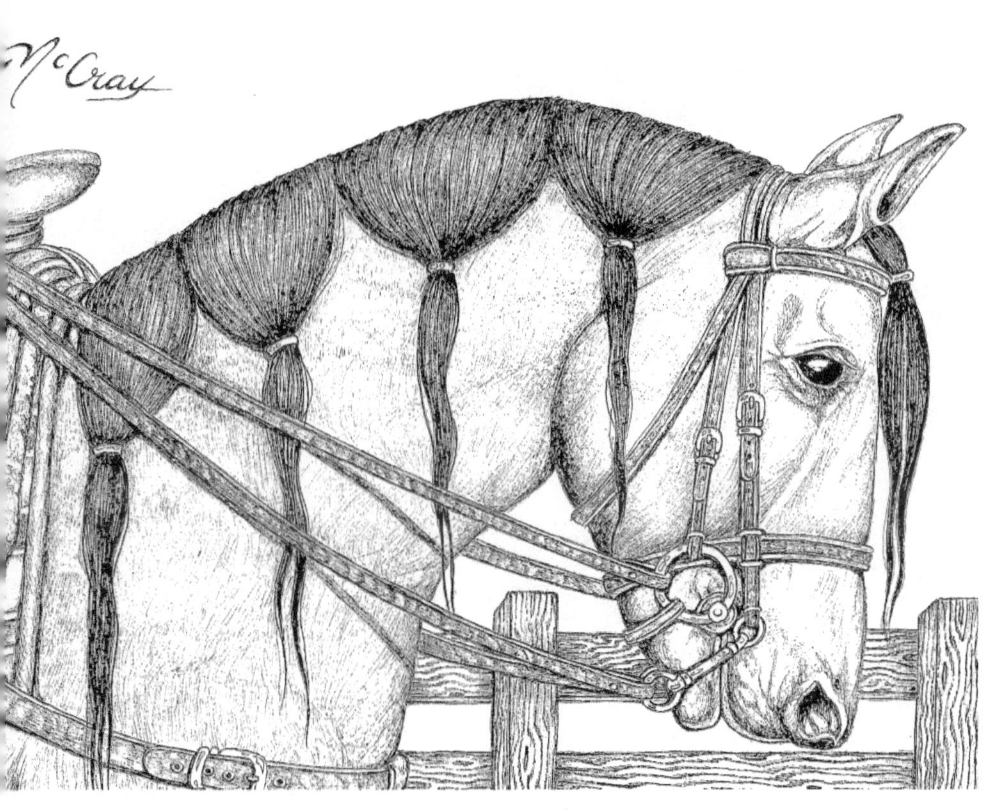
McCray

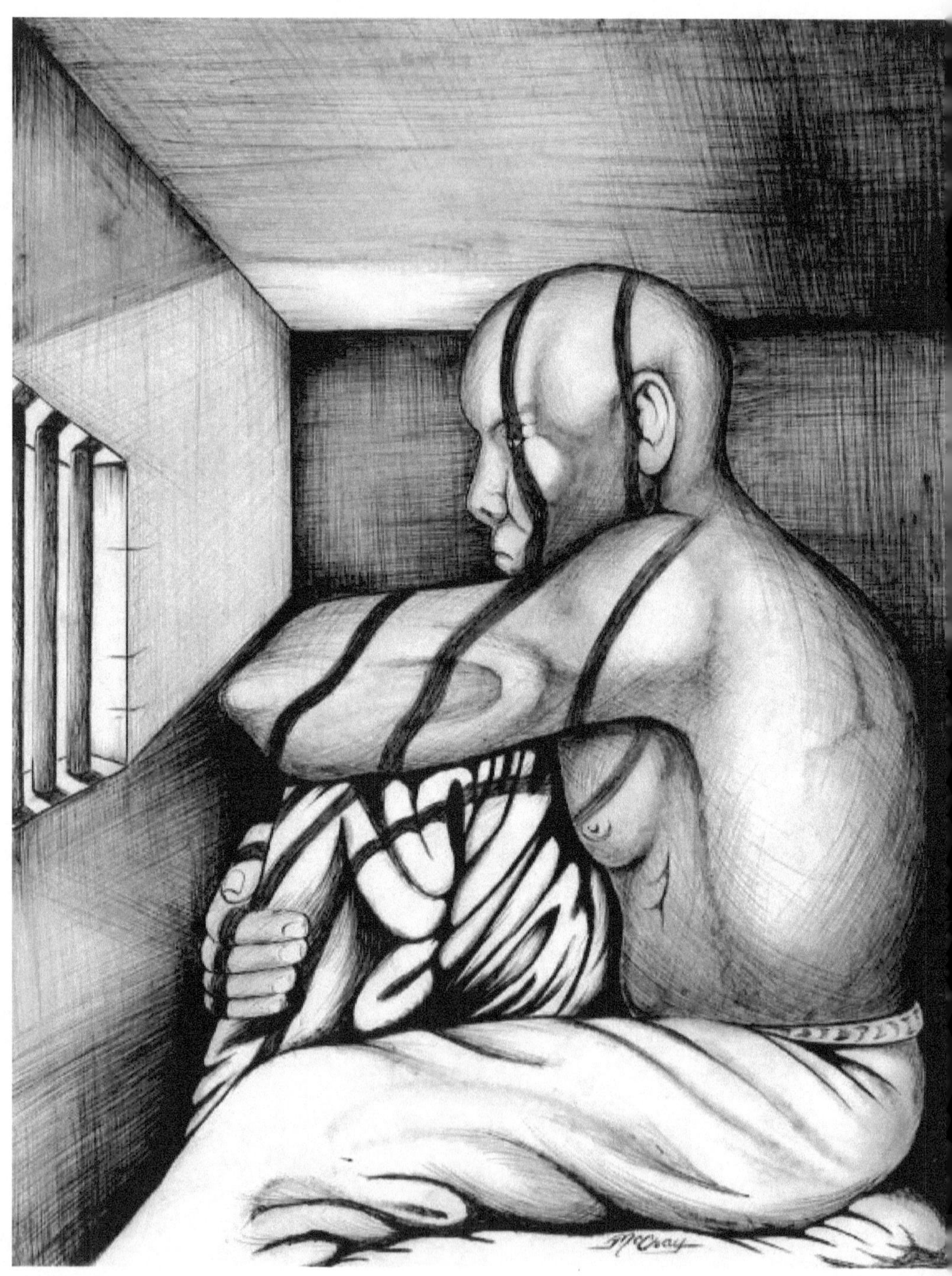

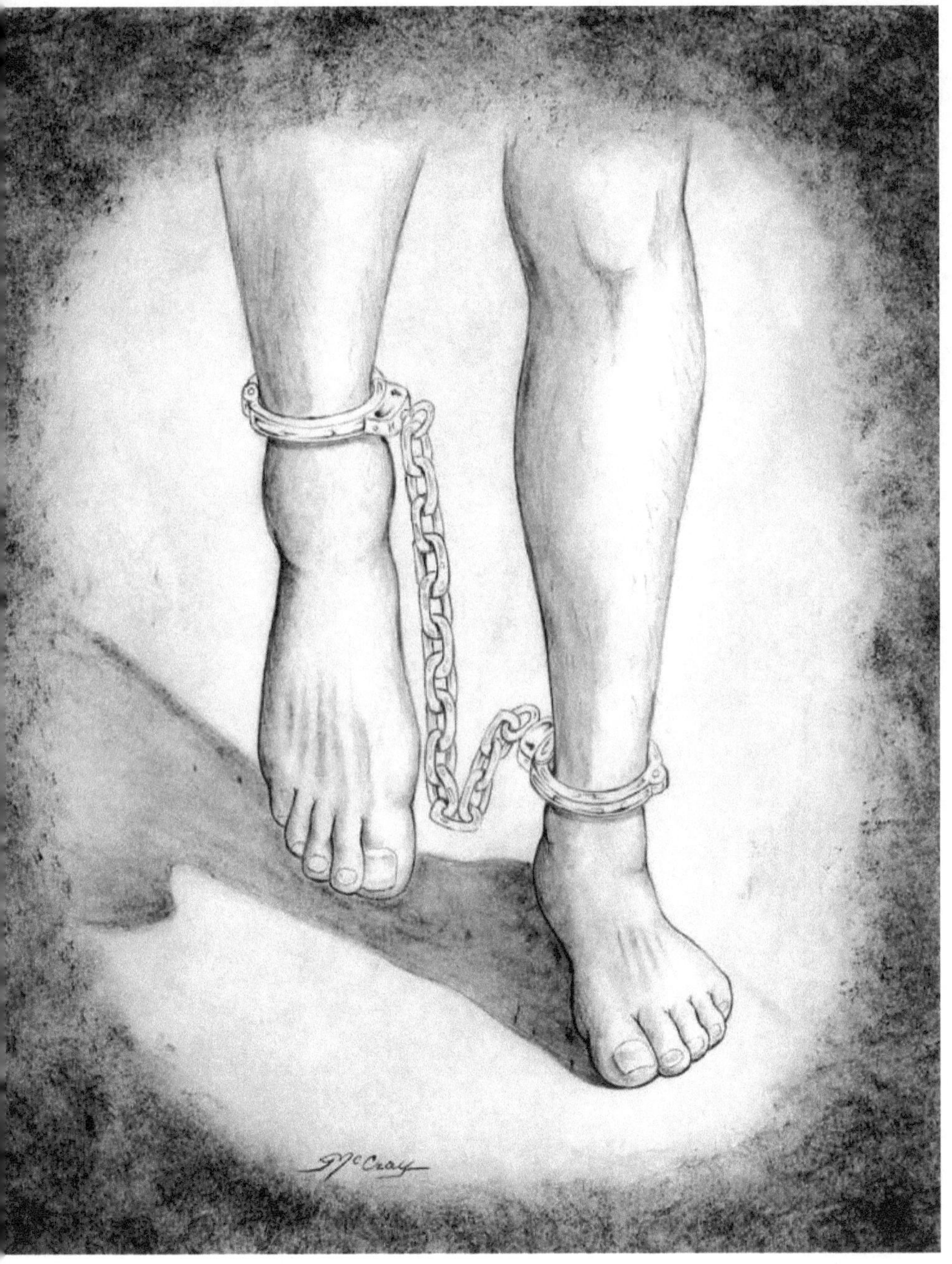

THE LETTERS
What will you do with them?

Now, if you have written to Death Row Inmates, what do you plan on doing with the letters you have gotten back?

Depending on who wrote you back, and what they wrote about, you may want to think about ways to preserve the letters. There is a market for letters and art work from certain people, there are those who collect things like letters from Killers for there own personal collection. But there are also organizations, and people who may like to document conditions on Death Row, or in prisons in general that may be interested in the letters once you are finished with them. If you have recived letters from Death Row or Killers, they are yours to do with what you wish. If you do not have a plan for the letters maybe think about what you would like to happen to them when you are done.

MY LETTERS

For me, I plan on holding onto most of my letters from Death Row and Serial Killers. As well as share some of the information about the conditions on Death Row. All of my letters have been scanned in so i have digital copies (that way if I wish to read them I do not have to chance messing up the physical letters) Some of these digital copies will eventually be shared, but for now they are safely being stored both digitally and the originals. If you do not know what to do with your letters or you wish to destroy them that is 100% your choice! I personally see the history in them, so I will preserve them and pass them on when I am finished with them.

YOUR LETTERS

Use these pages to write down what you wish to happen to any letters you may get from Death Row Inmates or Killers.

YOUR LETTERS

YOUR LETTERS

It is also a good idea to keep a log, it lets you know how long its been between letters.

SENT	RETURN
7/19 Ruben	8/3 Ruben
7/20 Brandon	8/3 Brandon
7/20 Michael	8/2 Michael
7/21 Edward	8/7 Edward
7/20 Roman	8/10 Roman
7/20 Jimmy	8/9 Jimmy
7/20 Shawn	8/2 Shawn

LETTER LOG

SENT	RETURN

SENT

RETURN

SENT	RETURN

SENT
RETURN

CARE PACKAGES

Some facilities do allow Care Packages. Each prison will have there own set of rules on this. However if this is something you would like to do, there are several options. If you do an Internet search on "How to send care packages to inmates" you will get a long list of companies that will offer to do this for you. You want to find the provider associated with the prison you will be sending to. Say you wish to send someone in San Quentin a care package; you would go to the California Dept. of Corrections page then go thru find a facility. Once you have located San Quentin, access the visitation and support information tab, and then the inmate package vendor's tab. Once here you will find a list of approved vendors for San Quentin.

IF YOU DO NOT use one of these venders and try to put together something your self the inmate **will generally not receive the package.** Some of the items that are available for purchase for inmates are hygiene items, food items, stationary, and clothing. There are still limits to what you can send, but this is an excellent way to show them you care, without providing them funds, as well as get them some items they may not have access to or funds to purchase.

Care packages can be refused or returned, for several reasons. Make sure your inmate hasn't lost privileges, hasn't already received a package this quarter and that they are authorized to receive the items prior to ordering a care package. Also keep in mind many prisons require you be on the inmates visiting list to send a care package.

COMPANIES THAT OFFER CARE PACKAGES

PRISON ADDICTIONS

Yes this is a thing!

YES! Drugs are in prisons!

But that is not the only thing Prisoners can and have found themselfs addicted to.

Physch Meds/Treatment

Relationships! Yes that is correct some they find in those very walls!

Pen/Pals, writing to outsiders, using them, having the affection and attention!

Jesus, yup you read that correctly! The bible has found itself the cause of addiciton too!

An addict can feel the same about anthing and become addicted to it when they can not get their hands on street/RX drugs Alcohol etc. Just because someone writes to you about Jesus, doesn't always mean they belive, it may just be the current addiction!

PERSONALITY

These change! Watch for changes in personality when reading letters! This is something i have seen a few times, when you tell them something they do not like, they can throw a hissy fit in the only way availible to them, thru their words.

They may go from totally normal letters from what seem like a long time friend, to when I was on the streets I was hard core, I did this drug and that drug, I robbed people, I hurt people, and so on.

You can end the letter writing with that individual or you can get them back on track! That choice is yours and yours alone.

You may read a letter from someone for the first time and see a man a woman a human.

They may be putting on a show or they could be 100% real in their words. It is up to you to figure that out.

Unless you keep the writing going full time long term, you may never know what anyone's intentions are in writing, including your own. But remember their and our personalities show thru in letter writing.

GIFTS

Yes some will send you Gifts, they wont be traditional gifts, or things you can get at any retail store. But for someone who has virtually nothing, anything they do have and posses, givin to someone else is a gift.

So if someone sends you a prison write up, they care, it may be all they have in this world. If you get a piece of artwork made by their hands, or even if they had someone else make it for you, they used what possibly little they had to get that for you. These things are gifts. Do not just throw them to the side but see them as that.

It is easy for you and I to take a piece of paper stick it in a cabinet or on a shelf and forget about it. For someone living in a cell, they have limited space, resourses and possessions. These things to us may not mean anything, but a 12 year old piece of paper from someone on the inside, that has kept this paper stored it and held onto it for 12 years means something.

For someone on the inside of that cell, to spend hours on a piece of art, maybe days, weeks, and send it to you, that means something!

So if any inmate sends you anything, including a letter, please remember they used what little they may have to do so.

THINGS I HAVE BEEN GIVEN

Drawings

Paper Art

Handmade Cards

Photos

Cards

Prison Write ups

Order forms

Visitation Forms

Court Paperwork

Doodles

Poetry

Jokes (lots of jokes)

WHAT HAVE YOU BEEN SENT?

Prison Recipes

Slushy

You take 2 frozen pops, (I like the grape ones) you can get them in the
 summer from the prison store and a soda, coke or a sprite.

You mix them together and you got a slushy.

Cheese Cake

Cookies, whatever kind you can get, you know for the crust.
Cream Cheese, vanilla creamer if you can get it, honey and
sugar. Thats all you need really.

You crush up the cookies and that is your crust, then you
mix all the other stuff together and put it in your crust.
Then your done! Cheese Cake, what you think we can't
cook?

Noodles

A pack of them noodles, a bag of doritoes like the size in the
vending machines, a can of tuna, and some cheese packets.

You cook up the noodles with your hot water, and then
when they are done, you drain out the water, add the packet
that came with it, i like the shrimp one, its good with tuna,
crush up the chips and then mix everything together. Its
better than when you just make noodles at home and only
put that packet of seasoning.

Prison Recipes

A place to keep ones given to you.

A PLACE TO WRITE OUT YOUR JOURNEY

How things are going how you are feeling about writing, and your process.

6'0"
5'0"
4'0"

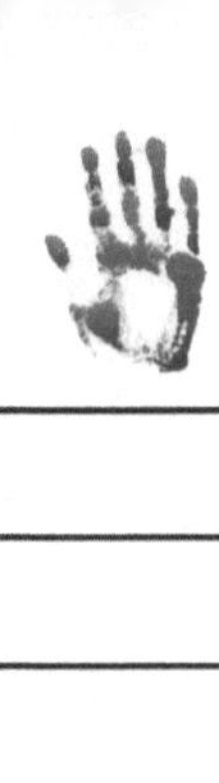

THANK YOU FOR SHARING MY JOURNEY IN WRITING TO KILLERS, LIFERS, AND THOSE ON DEATH ROW.

I AM AWARE THIS IS NOT SOMETHING JUST ANYONE CAN DO.

I DO TRULY BELIEVE NOT EVERYONE ON DEATH ROW DESERVES TO BE THERE, NOT EVERY ONE IN PRISON IS GUILTY AND NOT EVERYONE DESERVES TO BE ALONE.

WRITING TO DEATH ROW OR PRISON IN GENERAL WE NEVER KNOW WHO IS GOING TO WRITE BACK, THE MONSTER THAT THE NEWS AND MEDIA SAY, OR A LONELY PERSON JUST HAPPY THAT SOMEONE ANY ONE HAS REACHED OUT.

I PERSONALLY DO NOT USE PEN PAL SITES TO FIND INMATES TO WRITE TO! IF YOU DO THAT IS GREAT! I PREFER WRITING TO THOSE WHO DO NOT HAVE MEDIA COVERAGE AND ARE NOT LISTED ONLINE AS LOOKING FOR PEOPLE TO TALK TO. IT GIVES MORE IN-MATES A CHANCE TO HAVE CONTACT WITH THE WORLD OUTSIDE THOSE WALLS.

I hope all of you stay safe and
take care, until next time.

Sincerly,
Muriel A.

Each of these sites has provided me information you will find in this book. The information on the state's sites will be current and up to date, as one day the offenders listed in this book may no longer be on death row or may have been executed.

https://www.cdcr.ca.gov/capital-punishment/

https://www.tdcj.texas.gov/death_row/dr_offenders_on_dr.html

https://www.drc.ohio.gov/death-row

https://corrections.az.gov/public-resources/death-row

http://www.doc.sc.gov/news/deathrow.html

https://adc.arkansas.gov/death-row

https://deathpenaltyinfo.org/executions/execution-database

https://www.oregon.gov/doc/about/Pages/oregon-death-penalty.aspx

https://www.mdoc.ms.gov/Death-Row/Pages/Death-Row-Inmates.aspx

https://www.tn.gov/correction/statistics-and-information/death-row-facts/death-row-offenders.html

https://www.ncdps.gov/adult-corrections/prisons/death-penalty/death-row-roster